D1143592

The Call of the Wild

Jack London

Level 2

Retold by Tania Iveson
Series Editors: Andy Hopkins and Jocelyn Potter

Pearson Education Limited

Edinburgh Gate, Harlow,
Essex CM20 2JE, England
and Associated Companies throughout the world.

Pack ISBN: 978-1-4058-5207-4
Book ISBN: 978-1-4058-4274-7
CD-ROM ISBN: 978-1-4058-5057-5

First published 1903
First published by Puffin Books 1982
First published by Penguin Books 2000
This edition published 2007

1 3 5 7 9 10 8 6 4 2

Text copyright © Penguin Books 2000
This edition copyright © Pearson Education Ltd 2007
Illustrations by Mike McKeever

Set in 12/15.5pt A. Garamond
Printed in China
SWTC/01

Produced for the Publishers by AC Estudio Editorial S.L.

*All rights reserved; no part of this publication may be reproduced, stored in a retrieval system,
or transmitted in any form or by any means, electronic, mechanical, photocopying, recording or otherwise,
without the prior written permission of the Publishers.*

Published by Pearson Education Ltd in association with Penguin Books Ltd,
both companies being subsidiaries of Pearson Plc

Acknowledgements
Every effort has been made to trace the copyright holders and we apologise in advance for any
unintentional omissions. We would be pleased to insert the appropriate acknowledgement
in any subsequent edition of this publication.

We are grateful to the following for permission to reproduce photographs:
Page 58: University of Alaska
Page 59: Corbis (Mike Finn) (middle), Corbis (Reuters) (right), Empics (Mike Egerto

For a complete list of the titles available in the Penguin Active Reading series please write to
Pearson Longman office or to: Penguin Readers Marketing Department, Pearson Educa
Edinburgh Gate, Harlow, Essex CM20 2JE, England.

Contents

**ROTHERHAM LIBRARY &
INFORMATION SERVICES**

B48 635863

Askews

JF | £6.50

 | RO000064991

1.1 What's the book about?

1 Look at the picture on the front of this book and talk about it.
- What kind of dog is he?
- Where is he?
- Do you think he lives with a family or in the wild?

2 What do you think? Write these words below the pictures.

happy	sad	angry	excited	cold	warm
afraid	hungry	bored	dangerous	free	wild

......happy...... ....

....

....

....

1.2 What happens first?

Look at the picture and the words in *italics* on page 1. What do you think? Write the words in these sentences.

1 Buck is .... | a place   a person   a dog |

2 The weather looks .... | cold   warm   wet |

3 The house is in .... | Africa   Asia   North America |

4 The story begins in the .... | 1900s   1800s   1700s |

CHAPTER 1

To the North

Buck didn't know about the cold north, or gold—and he didn't know about Manuel.

Buck was a strong dog with a thick coat. He lived in a big house, Mr. Miller's place, in sunny California. There were tall trees around the house, and there was a pool, too. Buck was four years old, and the Millers were his family. He swam with the boys and walked with the women. He carried the babies on his back, and at night Buck sat at Mr. Miller's feet. There were other dogs at Mr. Miller's house, but Buck was the most important. He was the boss there, and he was very happy.

That year, 1897, was an exciting year. Some men found **gold** in the cold Arctic north of Canada, and a lot of people followed them there. Everybody wanted gold. And they wanted dogs—strong dogs with thick coats. The dogs had to pull the gold through the snow to towns and rivers.

But Buck didn't know about the cold north, or gold—and he didn't know about Manuel.

---

gold /gəʊld/ (n) *Gold* is expensive and yellow, and it comes from the ground.

Manuel worked for Mr. Miller, but he always wanted more money.

"I can sell Buck," he thought. "He's strong. Somebody will pay a lot of money for him."

One day, Mr. Miller was at work and the children were busy. Manuel put a **rope** around Buck's **neck** and left the house quietly. He met a man at a train station, and the man gave him money for the dog.

Buck didn't like this new man, and he started to **bark**. So the man pulled the rope around his neck very hard. This hurt Buck, and it made him angrier. He tried to fight the man, but the man pulled the rope again. The **pain** was very bad. Buck fell to the ground and his eyes closed.

He opened his eyes when a loud noise woke him. He was on a train! And there was that man again.

Buck was very hungry and thirsty, and he hated the rope around his neck. He jumped up and tried to **attack** the man. But the man was quick, and pulled the rope. Buck's neck hurt very badly. Then the man put him in a box.

"Crazy animal!" he said.

When they arrived in San Francisco, the man left Buck, in his box, at a bar.

The next morning, four other men arrived and put Buck in a car. He barked angrily at them, but they only laughed. He was in the box in the

---

rope /roʊp/ (n) When you put a *rope* around an animal, you can control it.
neck /nɛk/ (n) Your head sits on your *neck*.
bark /bɑrk/ (n/v) The *bark* of a dog is a short, loud noise.
pain /peɪn/ (n) When you feel *pain*, your body hurts.
attack /əˈtæk/ (n/v) An *attack* by a person or animal can hurt or kill you.

car for two days and two nights without food or water. He hated his box, and he hated the men. He wanted to kill somebody.

After a long time, they arrived in Seattle. Four men carried the box to a house and gave it to a man in a red shirt. This man had a **club** in his hand, and he looked at Buck.

"OK, I'll get you out of that box now," he said. He started to open the box carefully. Buck jumped up and barked. "Now, you crazy dog … " the man said.

And Buck really was crazy now. He had fire in his eyes, and he wanted to kill. He jumped at the man: one hundred and forty pounds of angry, crazy dog. But the man suddenly hit him very hard with the club. Buck fell to the ground, and barked. Then he attacked again. Again the man hit him, and again Buck fell to the ground. The pain was very bad.

Twelve times he attacked, and twelve times the man hit him. In the end, Buck couldn't stand up. He couldn't see or hear. He was almost dead.

club /klʌb/ (n) A *club* is large, heavy and usually made from wood. You hit people or animals with it.

"That will teach him!" shouted one of the men.

Buck slowly woke up and looked at the man with the red shirt. The man read from a paper on Buck's box.

"So your name's Buck. Buck, my boy," he said quietly, "we had a little fight and now we can forget about it. You know that I'm the boss. Be a good dog, and we'll be friends. I kill bad dogs. Do you understand?"

He brought Buck some food and water. Buck ate and drank quickly. He learned a lesson that day. He learned the lesson of the club, and he never forgot it.

One day, a small French-Canadian man came and looked at Buck. His name was Perrault.

"Wow! He's a big, strong dog. How much do you want for him?"

"Three hundred dollars," answered the man in the red shirt.

"This is a wonderful dog for the cold North," Perrault thought. "He's strong and his coat is thick and warm." He bought Buck and another dog, Curly, and he took the two dogs to a boat. Buck never saw the man in the red shirt or the warm South again.

On the boat, the two dogs met François, another French-Canadian. He and Perrault were kind and intelligent, and they understood dogs. Buck and Curly also met two other dogs, Spitz and Dave. Spitz took Buck's food, so Buck didn't like him. Dave was sad and unfriendly, and wasn't interested in anything. He only wanted to eat and sleep.

Day after day, the weather got colder. Then they arrived in Alaska, and François took the dogs off the boat. Buck walked on snow for the first time in his life.

2.1 Were you right?

Look back at your answers to Activity 1.2
on page iv. Then answer these questions.

1 Dog's name? ....

2 Place? ....

3 Date? ....

2.2 What more did you learn?

Put these in the right order. Write the numbers, 1–8.

○   Buck, Curly, Spitz, and Dave arrived in Alaska.

○   A man in a red shirt hit Buck hard with his club.

○   Manuel sold Buck to a man at a train station.

①   Buck lived happily with Mr. Miller and his family in California.

○   Buck went in a box by train to San Francisco.

○   Perrault bought Buck and took him north on a boat.

○   Men found gold in the north of Canada.

○   Four men took Buck to Seattle.

3 Language in use

Look at the sentences on the right. Then finish these sentences in the same way.

> It **made him angrier**.
>
> The weather **got colder**.

1 After five or ten years, the trees around the house got .... (tall)

2 People found gold in Alaska. It made .... (rich)

3 Buck didn't eat or drink on the train. He got ....
and .... (hungry, thirsty)

4 Buck was angry in the box, and the man's attack made .... (crazy)

5 Buck jumped at a man, and made the man .... (angry)

6 The train went north and the weather got .... (cold)

4 What's next?

Buck was a family dog in California. How will his new life in the North be different from his old life?

	life in California	life in the North
1 food	a lot	
2 bed	sleeps in the house	
3 work	doesn't work	
4 other dogs	friendly	
5 people	nice	

The Laws of the Wild

He was a wilder dog. On the cold, quiet nights,
Buck looked up and howled at the dark sky.

Buck's first day in this new, cold country was very bad. There were a lot of dangerous men and dogs everywhere.

This wasn't a sunny, easy life. Here, there was no **rest**. Buck had to be careful and he had to learn quickly.

These dogs and men weren't from the South. They were wild, and they followed the **law** of the club.

Buck's first new lesson, in this cold place, came quickly. Buck and Curly stood near a store, in one of the **camp**s. A new dog walked past them. Curly wanted to be friendly, so she barked quietly. Suddenly, the other dog turned around and attacked her. He hurt her face very badly. Many other dogs saw the attack and ran quickly to the two dogs. They stood and watched quietly. They all looked excited and interested, and Buck didn't understand.

Curly was very angry, so she jumped at this strange, unfriendly dog. But the dog attacked her again and jumped away quickly.

---

rest /rest/ (n) When you have a rest, you do nothing for a short time.
law /lɔ/ (n) A *law* is an important rule for everybody in that place.
camp /kæmp/ (n) People live in a *camp* in the country for a short time, and then they move to a new place.

Curly couldn't attack the other dog because he was very fast. Suddenly, he pushed Curly over and she fell on the ground. The other dogs ran at her, and Curly barked with pain. But she couldn't stand up and the other dogs attacked her again and again.

Buck couldn't move. Dogs in California never fought in this way. He looked at Spitz, and Spitz laughed. Then François jumped into the center of the crazy dogs and hit them with his club. He and three other men with clubs quickly moved the dogs away.

It all happened very fast, but in those two minutes Curly was dead.

Buck never forgot this attack. Spitz looked at Buck and he laughed again. From that time, Buck hated Spitz more than anything in life.

But then Buck had another **surprise**. François put a **harness** on him.

"I know you don't like this, Buck," said François. "I know it's new and strange for you. But you have to wear it. Then you can pull the **sledge**."

Buck didn't like this new thing around his neck, and he didn't like pulling the sledge.

surprise /səˈpraɪz, səˈpraɪz/ (n) When a friend plans a *surprise* for you, you don't know about it. When you learn about it, you are very *surprised*.
harness /ˈhɑrnɪs/ (n) You can control an animal when there is a *harness* over its head or body.
sledge /slɛdʒ/ (n) You can carry people or things across the snow on a *sledge*.

But François hit him when he did something wrong. And Spitz attacked him when he didn't run very fast. François shouted, "Mush!" and Buck had to run quickly. He then shouted, "Ho!" and Buck had to stop. In this way, Buck learned to pull the sledge.

"These are very good dogs," François said to Perrault, "Buck pulls very hard and he learns very quickly."

In the afternoon, Perrault bought three more dogs—Billie, Joe, and Sol-leks. Billie was a very friendly dog, but Joe was unfriendly. Sol-leks was the same—he wasn't interested in anybody or anything.

That night, Buck had another new problem. He wanted to sleep in a warm, dry place, so he tried to sleep with the men. But Perrault and François were surprised and angry, and they threw plates and cups at him. Buck ran away from them, and went back into the cold.

He was very unhappy; he didn't want to sleep outside. The snow was wet and cold, and the wind hurt him. He looked for the other dogs, but he couldn't see them anywhere! Suddenly, the snow moved under his feet and he jumped back. He started to bark angrily, but then he heard a friendly bark. Buck looked down and saw Billie.

Billie was a little ball under the snow and he was happy and warm. Then Buck understood. He quickly made a little bed under the snow, and he slept very well.

In the morning, Perrault and François bought three more dogs. Now they had nine dogs and they had to begin their trip. Buck was ready, and he was surprised by the excitement of the dogs. But he was most surprised by Sol-leks and Dave.

They were different dogs; suddenly they were happy, excited, and interested. They only loved two things—the harness and the work.

The days were very long and hard. They went past woods and across many large, icy rivers. It was difficult, but Buck worked hard. And at the end of every day he made his bed in the snow and fell asleep very quickly.

Buck was bigger than the other dogs and he was always hungry. François gave him a pound and a half of fish every night, but Buck always wanted more food. Also, Buck didn't eat as quickly as the other dogs, so they often took his fish away from him. After many days, Buck started to eat as fast as the others. And then he started to take other dogs' fish, too. One day, another dog, Pike, took some fish from the food box. Perrault didn't see him, but Buck watched carefully. The next day, Buck did the same thing.

Buck quickly learned the ways of **the wild**. And now he could live in this cold, unfriendly place. He wasn't the same dog—he was quicker, smarter, and stronger.

He was there, in the North, because Manuel wanted money. And men wanted gold. Now a new life began for Buck. He was a different dog—a wilder dog. On the cold, quiet nights, Buck looked up and **howl**ed at the dark sky.

the wild /ðə ˈwaɪld/ (n) In *the wild*, animals are free.
howl /haʊl/ (n/v) The *howl* of a dog is a long, high noise.

11

3.1 Were you right?

Look back at your answers to Activity 2.4. Then finish these sentences.

1 In California, Mr. Miller gave Buck food, but in the North

   he was always hungry.

2 In California, Buck slept in the Miller's house, but in Canada

   ....

3 In California he was a family dog, but in the North

   ....

4 The other dogs at the Miller's house were friendly, but in the North

   ....

3.2 What more did you learn?

Match the dogs on the right with the words in *italics*. Draw lines between them.

1 Some of the dogs killed *her*.   Spitz

2 *He* didn't like the harness.   Billie

3 *He* laughed when the dogs attacked Curly.   Curly

4 *They* loved working.   Buck

5 *He* attacked Buck when he didn't run fast.   Spitz

6 *They* made beds in the snow.   all the dogs

7 *He* was friendly with Buck.   Sol-leks and Dave

8 *He* was the biggest dog.   Buck

.3 Language in use

Look at the sentence on the right. Then finish these sentences in the same way.

> They all **looked excited** and **interested**.

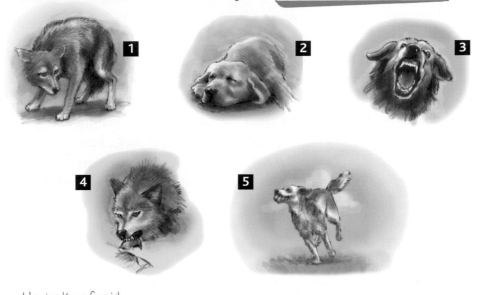

1 *He looks afraid.* ....

2 ....

3 ....

4 ....

5 ....

.4 What's next?

Look at the start of Chapter 3 and the words in *italics*. What do you think is going to happen? Discuss these questions.

1 Which two dogs are going to fight?

2 Why do dogs fight?

3 Which is the most important of the dogs?

4 Which dog will win the fight?

5 What will happen to the other dog?

A Bad Fight

*"Spitz is a dangerous dog. He really hates Buck.
One day he's going to kill him!"*

This new, wild animal in Buck was strong, but Buck's new life was very dangerous.

He never fought with the other dogs, but Spitz hated him.

Spitz was the most important dog. He knew the sledge best. He always taught the new dogs to work hard. And the other dogs were afraid of him. He was the strongest, the most intelligent and the most dangerous. He wanted to fight with Buck because every day Buck got stronger and more dangerous. But Spitz had to be the best, so he had to kill Buck.

One cold, windy evening, they stopped next to a river. Buck was very tired and he quickly made a warm bed in the snow. He wasn't happy when François shouted, "Buck, come eat your fish!" He didn't want to leave his warm bed, but he was very hungry. So he ran to the food box and quickly ate his dinner.

But when he turned around, he saw Spitz. The other dog was in Buck's bed. He looked at Buck and laughed. Buck barked at him, and the wild animal inside him went crazy.

He quickly jumped at Spitz. Spitz was very surprised because Buck was never angry.

François was also surprised when the two dogs started fighting.

"Fight him, Buck! You can win!" shouted François. "Get him, get Spitz, that bad dog!"

But the fight never finished, because Perrault shouted. Everybody heard the noise of Perrault's club and the cry of a dog. The camp was suddenly full of strange, thin dogs. There were eighty or a hundred of them, and they wanted food. The two men hit the dogs with their clubs, but the dogs didn't leave.

They found the food box, and they went crazy. The noise was very loud and the sledge dogs were afraid.

The strange dogs finished the food and then attacked the sledge dogs. They hurt them very badly. They hurt Dolly's neck and cut Dub's leg. They took out Joe's eye and almost cut off Billie's ear.

Billie cried in pain and ran away, over the icy river. The other sledge dogs followed Billie, and they all looked for a quiet place to sleep.

In the morning, the dogs walked slowly back to the camp.

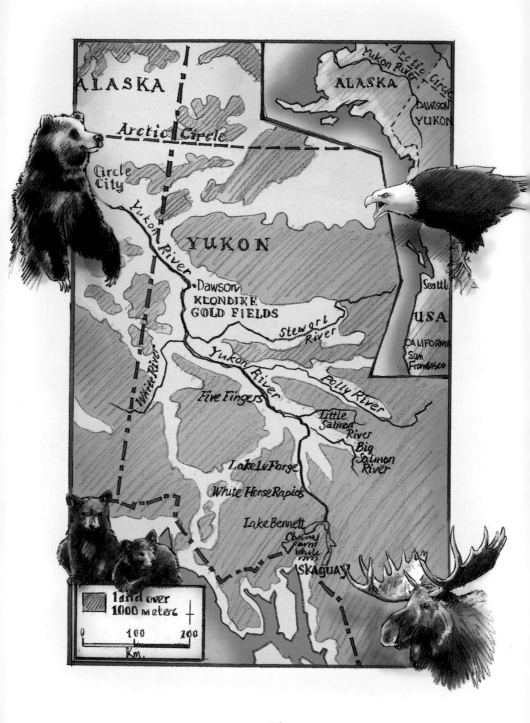

"Oh, my friends," said François sadly.

The dogs were in a lot of pain, and they looked very bad.

"Maybe you'll go crazy. Because those dogs attacked you, maybe you're crazy now. What do you think, Perrault?"

"No! They'll be fine," said Perrault. "We have many days of work so the dogs have to be all right!"

But the dogs weren't all right, and one morning, Dolly went crazy. She stopped in front of her harness and sat down. She howled loudly. Then she looked at Buck and jumped at him.

Buck was afraid! He didn't know any crazy dogs. And he liked Dolly—he didn't want to see this. He quickly ran away from Dolly, but she was only one jump behind him. He ran through the trees, across some ice and back to the river. Dolly barked crazily behind him, but she couldn't catch him.

"Buck, come here, boy. Come to me!" shouted François. Buck turned and ran back to the camp. He was very tired now and had a lot of pain in his legs.

"I'll have to help Buck," thought François, and he found his club. Buck ran past him and François's club came down very hard on Dolly's head.

Buck stopped and fell near the sledge. Spitz saw Buck and quickly attacked him. But François saw this and he hit Spitz with his club, many, many times.

"Spitz is a dangerous dog," said Perrault. "He really hates Buck. One day he's going to kill him!"

"But Buck's more dangerous," answered François. "I always watch him, and I know. One day he'll get very angry and he'll eat Spitz for dinner. He'll kill him easily. I know it."

◆

The weather got warmer and the trip got very difficult. The dogs couldn't fight—there was no time. The ice got very thin in some places and the sledge broke through it many times.

One time, when the ice broke, Buck and Dave fell into the icy water. They were almost dead when the two men pulled them out. The men

made a fire, and the dogs had to run
around it very quickly. They had to
get the thick ice off their coats.

Another time, Spitz went
through the ice and pulled
the other dogs in, too.
Then the ice broke behind
the sledge. Perrault had to
climb up a high **rock** next
to the river very quickly. He
took the rope from the dogs'
harnesses with him. Then
he pulled the dogs out of the
river, and onto the rock. With
the dogs' help, Perrault then
pulled the sledge onto the rock.
François climbed up after him.

Everybody was very cold and very tired. But they couldn't stay up on
the rock; they had to get back down to the river. So they walked to the
end of the rock and, slowly and carefully, François and Perrault took the
dogs back down. They only went a half of a kilometer that day.

Perrault wasn't happy, because this trip was too slow.

◆

So on the good days, the dogs had to work long hours. But Buck's feet
weren't as hard as the other dogs' feet. In sunny California, he never had
to walk on cold, hard ice and snow. So now he walked with a lot of pain.
One night, he couldn't get up and eat his fish.

François looked at Buck's tired feet. He wanted to help him, so he cut
off the tops of his **boots**. He made Buck four little dog-boots.

"Here, Buck," François said kindly. "These will help you."

---

rock /rɑk/ (n) *Rocks* are usually gray or brown and you find them on the ground.
boots /buts/ (n) You wear *boots* on your feet when you walk in rain or snow.

Buck loved his new little boots and he was happier after that. One morning, François forgot about Buck's boots. He harnessed the other dogs and then called Buck. But Buck didn't go to his harness and he didn't get up. Perrault and François found Buck and they laughed. Buck was on his back with his four feet up. François put Buck's boots on. Then the dog happily got up and walked to his harness.

"He really is a crazy dog," Perrault laughed.

After many more days on the river, they arrived in Dawson. It was a gray day, and everybody was very tired. There were men and dogs and sledges everywhere. Every day the dogs ran up and down the streets and pulled wood and gold for the men. The dogs worked very hard. They did the same work as horses. And every night, at twelve and at three, the dogs howled at the night sky.

They sang their strange song, and Buck loved to sing with them. It was a very old song—a song from a younger world. And when Buck howled, he howled with the pain of his wild fathers.

Seven days later, they left Dawson. The dogs were strong now, and the fighting quickly began again.

Buck had small fights with Spitz every day, and he always fought him in front of the other dogs. Now Buck was stronger and more dangerous than Spitz, and the other dogs could see this. They stopped liking Spitz. Other dogs began to fight with Spitz, too. They weren't afraid of him and they didn't listen to him. So the dogs began to work badly and they didn't pull the sledge well.

François got very angry at his dogs.

"You stupid dogs!" he shouted, and he hit them again and again. But nothing helped. The dogs didn't stop fighting.

One night, after dinner, a dog found a small animal. The animal jumped up and ran away very quickly. The sledge dogs saw it and they quickly ran after it. Buck was in front of the other dogs. He was very excited. He wanted to catch the animal and kill it. He ran and ran. But the animal was always one jump in front. Buck was very happy.

Spitz quietly left the dogs and ran a different way. Buck didn't see him.

Suddenly Spitz jumped out in front of the animal. It couldn't turn around, and Spitz's big teeth killed it quickly.

The other dogs howled and barked. But Buck didn't bark and he didn't stop. He ran at the white dog, and Buck and Spitz began their last, dangerous fight.

Spitz fought very well, and he attacked Buck again and again. Buck tried to push him onto the ground, but Spitz always jumped away very quickly. After some minutes, Buck was in a lot of pain. He had many cuts, but Spitz was fine. Buck was very tired, and the other dogs watched him carefully. Then Buck jumped at Spitz again. His teeth closed around Spitz's leg, and Spitz cried loudly. With a quick jump, Buck broke Spitz's leg.

Spitz was now in a lot of pain, but he tried hard to stand up. Then Buck started the last attack. He could see and feel the other dogs. They waited and watched. They wanted one of the two dogs to fall. Buck jumped up and hit Spitz hard. Spitz cried and fell. The other dogs quickly attacked him. Buck sat down and watched. He was very tired. But he felt good, because now he was the most important dog.

4.1 Were you right?

Look back at your answers to Activity 3.4. Then look again at this picture. What happened before this? What happened next? Tell the story to other students.

4.2 What more did you learn?

Write one word in each sentence.

1 Buck went to the food box and ....Spitz............ took his bed.

2 François was .... when Buck attacked Spitz.

3 .... or more wild dogs attacked the sledge dogs.

4 Joe lost one of his .... in the attack.

5 After that, ... went crazy and she attacked Buck.

6 Buck's feet were cold, so François made him little ....

7 Spitz killed a .... animal.

8 Buck attacked Spitz and .... his leg.

.3 Language in use

Look at the sentence on the right. Why did Spitz have to kill Buck? Complete these first parts of sentences with the second parts of sentences in the box.

> Spitz had to be the best, **so** he had to kill Buck.

1 Spitz took Buck's bed, so ......*A*......

2 Buck and the other dogs ran away because ....

3 François hit Dolly because ....

4 Buck and Dave fell into the water because ....

5 One day they only went half a kilometer, so ....

6 There was a lot of wood and gold in Dawson, so ....

7 After his last fight with Spitz, Buck felt good because ....

A Buck attacked him.	**D** eighty to a hundred dogs attacked the camp.
B the ice broke.	
C now he was the most important dog.	**E** she attacked Buck.
	F the dogs worked very hard.
	G Perrault wasn't happy.

4.4 What's next?

Look at the pictures in Chapter 4. Where is Spitz? What is going to happen next? How is Buck going to feel? What do you think? Discuss these questions and make notes.

Notes

The New Boss

François put his arms around Buck's neck and he cried.
Buck never saw the two men again.

"Hey, what did I say? I was right. Buck is a very dangerous dog," François said the next morning. He couldn't find Spitz anywhere, and Buck had many cuts on him.

Perrault looked at Buck's cuts and said, "Yes, but Spitz fought hard."

"And Buck fought harder," answered François. "Now the sledge will go faster. Without Spitz, there will be no more problems. I know I'm right."

Then Perrault put the bags onto the sledge and François put the dogs into their harnesses. Buck walked to Spitz's harness and waited. But François didn't see him and brought Sol-leks to the same place. Buck jumped at Sol-leks angrily, and Sol-leks had to move away.

"Ha!" François laughed. "Look at Buck! He killed Spitz, and now he wants his job! Go away, Buck!" he shouted, but Buck didn't move. Then François pulled Buck by his neck and put Sol-leks in Spitz's harness. Buck barked angrily, but he moved. Sol-leks was afraid of Buck and he didn't want to make Buck angry. So, when François turned around, Buck easily pushed Sol-leks away again.

François was angry now. "Buck—you bad dog! You move away now!" he shouted, and he took his club. Buck remembered the man in the red shirt and he walked away.

When François brought Sol-leks back, Buck didn't bark.

"OK, now you, Buck. Come here and get into your harness," François said.

But Buck walked away from him. François followed, but Buck didn't stop.

François looked down at the club in his hand. "Oh, I understand. You're afraid of this. All right, I'll put it on the ground—look. Now, come to me."

But Buck wasn't afraid of the club and he didn't go to François. He wanted to be in Spitz's harness. He was the best dog now and he didn't want to go back to his old harness. He walked away again. He didn't leave the camp, but François couldn't get near him.

After an hour, François sat down. He looked at Perrault and smiled. Then he looked back at Buck.

"OK, Buck, you win!" And he took Sol-leks out of Spitz's place.

Buck laughed and walked to the sledge. François put him in his new harness.

"Mush!" François shouted, and the sledge started to move. François watched Buck carefully. "I don't think Buck can do Spitz's job." François thought. But he was wrong.

After some kilometers, François thought, "Wow! Buck is better than Spitz! He's faster, stronger, and more intelligent than Spitz. Spitz was the best dog, but now Buck is better!"

Buck quickly stopped the fighting between the other dogs.

He was the new boss now, and the other dogs were afraid of him. They listened to him and worked hard for him. François and Perrault were surprised and very happy.

"Buck is the best sledge dog in the North." François said. "Somebody will pay a thousand dollars for him! What do you think, Perrault?"

"Yes, you're right," he said. Perrault was very happy with Buck's work, too.

Perrault was also very happy with this trip. The ice was hard, and there was no new snow. It wasn't too cold. Every day, for fourteen days, they ran 20 kilometers. And at the end of the second week, they could see Skaguay.

But when they arrived at Skaguay, François and Perrault's plans changed. They had to leave Skaguay and the Yukon.

They had to sell the dogs quickly. François put his arms around Buck's neck and he cried. Buck never saw the two men again.

◆

A Scottish man bought the sledge dogs. He and some other men worked for the Canadian Mail Company. They carried people's letters to them. The next day, they took the sledge back to Dawson, and it was hard work for the dogs. The sledge was very heavy and the snow was very thick. Buck didn't like this new job, but he always worked hard. And the other dogs had to work hard, too.

On this trip, Buck only liked one thing. He liked to sit by the fire at night, before he went to bed. He often thought about Curly and his fight with Spitz. Sometimes he remembered Mr. Miller's house in California. But he wasn't sad. He didn't want to go back to Mr. Miller's big house and the warm sun. He had a new home now, and a new life. This life was hard, but good.

After many more days and nights, they arrived in Dawson. Now the dogs were very tired. They were very thin, and they wanted a long rest.

But they only had two days' rest, and then they had to start again. The dogs couldn't run fast, and the men weren't happy. And it snowed every day, so the sledge got heavier and heavier. It was the dogs' third trip back to Skaguay. And day after day, they got weaker and weaker.

Dave had the biggest problem. Sometimes the sledge stopped suddenly, and Dave cried with pain. The men looked at him carefully, but they couldn't find the problem. Something was wrong inside Dave, but they couldn't help him.

After three days, Dave was very weak, and he fell to the ground in his harness many times. The Scottish man stopped the sledge and took him out of his harness. He wanted to give Dave a rest, but this made the dog angry. Dave was in a lot of pain, but he had a job. It was his work, and Dave hated to see another dog in his harness. The sledge started to move again, and Dave ran next to the other dogs. Running was very difficult in the thick snow. He cried and barked with pain.

He was also very weak, and he fell down in the snow. He howled sadly, and started to walk slowly behind the sledge.

The dogs had to have a short rest, so the men stopped. They watched Dave. He walked slowly and carefully to the sledge. He stopped next to Sol-leks and didn't move away.

One man said, "Some dogs die because they can't work. Sledge dogs love their work. And when they can't pull the sledge, they don't want to live."

The Scottish man listened and then said, "I think Dave is going to die. But he can die in his harness. Then he'll die happy."

So the men put Dave back into his harness, and the sledge started again. Dave was happy in his harness, but the pain was very bad. He fell many times, and one time, the sledge went over his legs. But he stayed in his harness and night came. The men stopped and made their camp. Dave fell down in the snow next to the sledge. They gave the dogs their fish, but Dave couldn't eat.

In the morning, Dave couldn't get up. He tried to go to his harness, but he couldn't move his legs. The men waited for a short time, but then they had to leave. The sledge moved away from the camp and Dave howled sadly.

The sledge went behind some trees, and the Scottish man stopped the dogs. "I have to help Dave," he thought. "He'll die slowly in the cold snow, and I don't want that. He was a good dog."

He walked back to Dave, and the other men stopped talking. Then they heard the sound of a gun. The Scottish man came back quickly and shouted, "Mush!" The sledge moved away fast. But Buck knew, and every other dog knew. They understood the sound of the gun. And now Dave had no more pain.

5.1 **Were you right?**

Look back at your notes for Activity 4.4. Then put the right words in the story.

After the fight with Spitz, ...Buck........ was the most important dog. He took the place of Spitz at the .... of the sledge. The other dogs were .... of him. So François and Perrault were very .... with his work. But then they sold the dogs to a .... man. The dogs carried .... for the new men, in the thick snow. Some dogs became very weak, and the men had to kill ....

5.2 **What more did you learn?**

Write a sentence under each picture. Then put them in order, 1–4.

3 Language in use

Look at the sentences on the right. Then finish these sentences in the same way.

> He's **faster, stronger,** and more intelligent.
>
> He was **the best** dog now.

1 Buck was ....*bigger*........ than Spitz. (big)

2 ....
.... (strong)

3 ....
.... (intelligent)

4 ....
.... (dangerous)

5 Buck was .... of the dogs. (heavy)

6 ....
.... (good)

7 ....
.... (fast)

8 ....
.... (important)

4 What's next?

In the next chapter, the Scottish man sells the dogs again. Look at the start of Chapter 5 and the words in *italics*. Then look at the pictures in this chapter. What is happening? Write one sentence about each picture.

1 ....

2 ....

3 ....

4 ....

5 ....

A Bad Trip

The dogs began to die because they were tired, weak,
and very hungry.

The Canadian Mail sledge, with Buck and the other dogs, arrived in Skaguay. They looked and felt very tired. Buck was very thin. The dogs' feet had cuts on them and they couldn't run. After thirty days without a rest, they were very weak.

"Come, my friends," said the driver. "This is the end. Now we'll have a long rest—a very long rest."

But there were letters in Skaguay for the men in the North, and the mail sledge had to leave again. The dogs only had a three-day rest. They were tired and weak, and now they couldn't pull the heavy sledge. The men had to buy new, strong dogs, so the Scottish man sold Buck and the other dogs. He didn't ask for a lot of money because the dogs couldn't work very hard.

◆

Two American men, Charles and Hal, bought the tired dogs and their harnesses. Charles was forty-five years old and he had weak, watery eyes. Hal was a younger man of about twenty. He wasn't a kind man.

He always carried a gun and a big knife with him. The two men looked strange in the North, and they didn't understand life there.

Hal and Charles took Buck and the other dogs to their new camp. Buck saw a woman, Mercedes, there, and a very large sledge. Hal put the dogs into their harnesses and the dogs waited. The men put a lot of bags and boxes onto the sledge, and it got heavier and heavier.

A man walked past and looked at their sledge.

"You have a very big, heavy sledge there," he said to Hal. "It's too heavy. Do you really think it will move?"

"Of course—now go away!" shouted Hal, and he took out his club. "Mush! Go! Move!" he shouted to the dogs. The dogs jumped and tried to move the sledge. But it was too heavy and they couldn't move it.

"You stupid dogs! You aren't pulling hard!" shouted Hal. "I'll kill you!" And Hal started to hit the weak dogs with his club.

Some men came and watched Hal.

"Those dogs are tired. They want a rest," said one man.

"Be quiet!" shouted Hal, and he started to hit the dogs again.

Another man watched angrily. "Those poor dogs," he thought. "That man is very stupid, but I have to help those dogs." So he shouted to Hal, "Break the ice under the sledge. The dogs want to work hard, so don't hit them. Help them, and your sledge will move."

Hal didn't want to listen to the man, but his dogs couldn't move. So he broke the ice, and the sledge slowly moved down the street. But the road suddenly turned left and the large sledge fell over. Bags and boxes went everywhere. Then the harnesses broke from the sledge, and the dogs ran away.

Many nice people came and helped Hal, Charles, and Mercedes. They found their things and brought the dogs back.

One man said, "You'll have to buy more dogs. Your sledge is very heavy."

So Charles bought more dogs, and now they had fourteen animals. They started again, and the men felt happy and important.

The heavy sledge moved slowly down the street. The dogs worked as hard as they could.

The trip back to Dawson was very bad. Hal, Charles, and Mercedes fought every day. They didn't have any plans and they didn't know about this cold country. They started late in the morning and finished early in the afternoon. So they didn't go many kilometers in a day. They hated the cold, the snow, and the Yukon.

They also didn't know about dogs, so they didn't bring much food for them. The dogs began to die because they were tired, weak, and very hungry. In one week, six dogs died, and the other dogs were almost dead.

It was beautiful spring weather. The sun came up early and went down late every day. The birds sang, and the trees were green again. The ice on the river started to break. But through these wonderful days, with new life everywhere, the two men, the woman, and the dogs walked. They didn't enjoy the spring. They thought only of the hard work and the pain.

Buck and the other dogs had no life in them when they arrived, one evening, at John Thornton's camp. When the sledge stopped, every dog fell down in the snow. They looked dead.

"What's the best way to Dawson?" Hal asked Thornton.

Thornton looked at the sledge and thought, "I know these people. They're stupid. I know they won't listen to me. But I want to help those dogs."

"The weather is warmer now," he said to Hal, "and the ice is very thin. Don't walk across this river to Dawson now."

"Some people in Skaguay said the same thing, and we're here. You're wrong—the ice is thick. We're going to finish our trip. We will get to Dawson," Hal answered.

Thornton didn't stop them. They didn't want to hear his words. They didn't understand the North.

Hal shouted to his dogs, "Get up, you stupid animals! Move! Get up, Buck!"

But Buck didn't get up. So Hal took his club and hit him hard. Buck stayed on the ground. Hal hit him again and again. Buck didn't want to get up.

On this trip the ice felt dangerous under his feet. It felt different, and many times on the last river, he was afraid. He was very, very tired and he couldn't get up. The club didn't hurt very much now and Buck started to die. He could hear the club, but now he couldn't feel it.

Suddenly, Thornton attacked Hal. Hal fell to the ground. Thornton stood over Buck and said angrily, "You hit that dog again, and I'll kill you!"

"It's my dog," answered Hal. "Get out of my way or I'll kill you. We're going to Dawson and you aren't going to stop us!"

Thornton stood between Hal and Buck. He didn't move. Then Hal took out his long knife. But Thornton quickly hit Hal on the hand and the knife fell to the ground. Thornton hit Hal again. Then he took the knife and quickly cut Buck's harness.

Hal couldn't fight Thornton. He was tired, and Buck was almost dead. He didn't want him now.

Minutes later, the heavy sledge, with five tired dogs, Hal, Charles and Mercedes, went down to the river. Buck watched them, and Thornton sat down next to Buck. He felt Buck's legs and his back.

"This animal will have to have a lot of food and rest," he thought. "I hope he doesn't die."

The sledge moved slowly across the river. Suddenly, the thin ice broke and the sledge fell into the cold water. The dogs barked and Mercedes shouted. Then the dogs and the people quickly went under the ice. Buck never saw them again. Thornton looked at Buck, and Buck looked back at him.

"Oh, Buck," Thornton said quietly.

6.1 Were you right?

Look back at your answers to Activity 5.4. Then write these words in the box.

Buck	the Scottish man	Mercedes
Thornton	the sledge dogs	Charles and Hal

dead	living
Mercedes	

6.2 What more did you learn?

Are these sentences right (✓) or wrong (✗)? Change the wrong sentences and write them in the box below.

✓ **1** The Scottish man sold the dogs for very little money.

◯ **2** Hal was a kind man.

◯ **3** Charles and Hal's sledge was very light.

◯ **4** Hal broke the ice under the sledge for the dogs.

◯ **5** Thornton liked Charles and Hal.

◯ **6** The weather got warmer because it was summer.

◯ **7** Thornton hit Buck with a club.

◯ **8** Thornton cut Buck's harness and took him away.

Right answers

3 Language in use

Look at the sentence on the right. Then finish these sentences in the same way.

> It was **too heavy** and they couldn't move it.

1 She was .... *too tired* .... (tired)

She .... *couldn't walk* ....

2 It was .... (expensive)

She ....

3 The dog was .... (fast)

The man ....

4 They were .... (late)

They ....

.4 What's next?

Buck is now very sick. Do you think Thornton will be a good friend to Buck? Will Buck die? How will the story end? Discuss these questions with other students and make notes below.

Notes

CHAPTER 6

For the Love of a Man

"Some men like to fight. And when somebody hurts Thornton, Buck will go crazy."

John Thornton had bad feet from an accident in the winter before Buck came. So his friends made a camp for him, and they left him by the river.

"We're going to Dawson. But we'll be back for you when the weather's warmer. Have a long rest here and get better," they said.

In the camp, Buck sat and watched the river. He listened to the songs of the birds, and he slowly got stronger and stronger. They all got stronger—Buck, Thornton, and his other dogs, Nig and Skeet—and they waited for Thornton's friends.

Skeet was a small, friendly dog, and she was a little doctor to Buck. Every morning, after breakfast, she carefully washed Buck's cuts. Nig was a very large, black dog and he was also friendly. They were good friends and they played games every day. And Buck slowly learned a new lesson. He learned about love. For the first time in his life, he felt strong love—for Thornton. This wonderful man took him away from Hal, and he helped him. He was kind and friendly, and he never hit him. Thornton's dogs were his children and he talked to them every day. Buck loved Thornton's talks with him. He barked at him.

"Wow, Buck," Thornton laughed. "I think you can speak!"

Buck's love for Thornton got stronger and stronger. He loved Thornton more than anything in life.

◆

Thornton's friends, Hans and Pete, arrived in the camp with their boat.

In the beginning, Buck didn't like these strange men, but then he saw Thornton's love for his friends.

So Buck walked to them when they called him. And he didn't bark angrily at them. But Buck's love was only for Thornton, and Hans and Pete could see this.

One day, the two men watched Thornton and Buck.

"Buck really loves Thornton," Pete said. "But I'm afraid. You know the men in the North. Sometimes they get angry easily and some men like to fight. And when somebody hurts Thornton, Buck will go crazy."

"Yes," answered Hans. "In Thornton's next fight, Buck will kill the other man."

It was at Circle City, in December, when Pete remembered those words. Thornton and his friends were in a bar. "Black" Barton was in the bar, too. He was a large, angry man. Barton wanted to fight with somebody, so he started to speak angrily to a smaller man. The man was afraid.

Thornton watched the two men. "Oh, no, there's going to be a fight," he thought. "And this won't be a good fight, because Barton is bigger than that other man. I'll have to do something."

So Thornton went to Barton and spoke quietly to him. Barton turned around and hit Thornton very hard in the face.

The people in the bar heard a loud angry bark. Then a large dog quickly jumped up and ran at Barton. Barton put up his arm and Buck attacked it. Buck and Barton fell to the floor. Buck was on top of the man. He was very angry, and he attacked Barton again. This time, he hurt his neck very badly and Barton shouted with pain. Then some men pulled Buck off Barton and they took the dog outside.

A doctor came and looked at Barton's neck.

"He's got a very bad cut, but he's going to live," he said.

A man said, "Yes, but Buck's dangerous. He almost killed that man! We'll have to kill him."

"No, we can't do that!" said another man. "Buck attacked Barton because Barton hit Thornton. He's a good dog, and he helped his friend."

So nobody was angry with Buck. But other people in Alaska heard about this wonderful, strange dog and his great love for Thornton.

◆

At the end of the next summer, Buck showed his love for Thornton again. Hans, Pete, and Thornton wanted to take their boat down a fast river. Hans and Pete stood next to the river when Thornton was in the boat. Buck didn't like this river, and he watched Thornton very carefully.

Suddenly, the boat moved very quickly through the water and it hit a rock. The boat turned over and Thornton fell into the cold river. He quickly went under the fast water, and the river carried him away.

Buck jumped into the water and swam to his friend. When he came near, Thornton put his arms around Buck's neck. Then Buck tried to swim to Hans and Pete. They could pull Thornton out. But the water was very fast, and it pushed Thornton and Buck quickly down the river.

"You can't pull me to Hans and Pete!" Thornton shouted to Buck. He caught a large rock and pushed Buck away. "Go Buck! Go! You have to get out of the river!"

Buck didn't want to leave his friend, but he slowly swam to Hans and Pete.

The two men pulled the wet dog out of the river. They had to help
Thornton quickly, so they ran fast to a place above Thornton.

Then they put a rope around Buck and he quickly jumped into
the cold water again. But the water was too strong and it carried Buck

past Thornton. Hans and Pete had to pull Buck out of the river again fast, before he hit the dangerous rocks. When they got Buck out of the water, he looked dead. There was a lot of water in his nose and mouth. Hans and Pete hit the water out of him, but he couldn't see very well.

"Help, help! I'm going down," shouted Thornton.

Buck heard his friend's cry and jumped up. He felt very bad, but he had to help Thornton. Hans, Pete, and Buck quickly ran back to the place above Thornton. They put the rope around Buck's neck again, and he jumped in.

The water was very strong and very cold, but Buck didn't stop. Buck swam to Thornton, and Thornton caught him around his neck. Hans and Pete pulled the rope very hard, and slowly Buck and Thornton moved nearer to them. But they went under the water many times, and they hit many hard rocks.

Then, suddenly, they were on the ground next to the river. They looked dead and they had a lot of cuts on them. Buck couldn't move and he couldn't open his eyes.

When Thornton woke up, he wanted to see Buck. He sat up and saw his beautiful dog on the ground near him.

"Is he dead?" he quickly asked Pete.

"No," Pete answered, "but he's in a lot of pain and he can't walk."

"OK," said Thornton quietly, "we can't go down this river now. We'll stay here. And when Buck's well, we'll take the boat down the river again."

After many weeks, Buck got better and they all went down the river to Dawson.

◆

That winter, at Dawson, Buck did another wonderful thing for Thornton.

Hans, Pete, and Thornton were in a bar, one afternoon, with other men.

Suddenly, one man said, "I have a very strong dog. I think he can pull a sledge with two hundred kilos of sugar on it!"

Another man, Matthewson, said, "Ha! That's nothing. My dog can pull a sledge with three hundred kilos of sugar on it."

"Now that's nothing," said Thornton. "My Buck can pull a sledge with four hundred and fifty kilos of sugar on it!"

"And walk a hundred meters with it?" asked Matthewson.

"Yes, and walk a hundred meters," answered Thornton coldly.

"Let's see this, and I'll give you a thousand dollars. Or you have to give me a thousand dollars. OK?" said Matthewson. He put a large bag of gold on the table. "And here it is. I have a sledge outside, now, and it has four hundred and fifty kilos of sugar on it."

Nobody spoke, and Thornton's face went very red.

"Oh, no!" he thought. "Can Buck pull four hundred and fifty kilos of sugar?"

He looked at the faces around him. And then he saw an old friend, Jim O'Brien.

"Can you give me a thousand dollars?" he asked quietly.

"Yes, of course," answered his good friend.

Everybody walked quickly out of the bar. They were excited. They talked about Buck's test and about the money.

Thornton brought Buck to Matthewson's sledge, and put on his harness. Buck looked beautiful. He was young and strong. Thornton sat down next to Buck and put his arms around his neck. Then he put his hands on Buck's face and looked into his eyes.

"Do this for my love, Buck. Do this for me," he said quietly.

Then Thornton stood up and walked away from his dog.

"Now, Buck ... GO!" he shouted.

Buck jumped up and pulled hard,
but it was a very difficult job. Buck pulled and pulled. Nobody spoke.
Slowly, the sledge began to move. It moved one centimeter, and then
two centimeters. And then it started to move across the snow. Thornton
walked behind the sledge and shouted, "That's it, Buck. You're a strong
dog. You can do it. Go, go!"

Buck felt tired, but he didn't stop. Slowly, he walked to the end of the
hundred meters. Everybody went crazy. They shouted and jumped. They
were happy and excited. They talked about Buck, the most wonderful
dog in Alaska.

Thornton sat down next to Buck and put his hands on Buck's head.

"I love you, you crazy, wonderful dog," he said happily.

CHAPTER 7

The Call of the Wild

In the woods, he wasn't a sledge dog. In the trees,
he was a wild animal—quick and careful.

When Buck walked past that hundred meter line, he showed his strong love for Thornton. But he also won a thousand dollars. And now the three men could begin a new trip. They wanted to go to new and strange places, in the East. They wanted to leave the towns and cities, and to find some gold.

When they said goodbye, their friends weren't happy. "Be careful!" their friends said. "You'll be in the wild for months, and it will be dangerous."

But Thornton, Hans, and Pete weren't afraid. With a sledge, some dogs, and guns, they could live anywhere in the wild. And they could live happily away from other people for a long time.

Month after month they walked. They went down new rivers and slept on new mountains. They felt strange, new winds. Every day they caught fish or small animals for food, and Buck loved this. He loved catching his food and he loved going to these new and exciting places.

One day, they found a road through the woods. But it began nowhere and ended nowhere. Another day, they found an old house in the middle of some trees. They found a gun and an old bed inside, but no people. They saw summer, fall, winter, and then spring again.

And at the end of their trip, they found a wonderful place between two small mountains. There was a small river, and at the bottom of this river the men could see gold.

The men worked hard, day after day. They took the gold from the bottom of the river and put it into large bags. And every day, they got richer and richer. But the dogs had no work, so Buck started to take long walks in the woods.

He didn't understand this new place, but he felt very happy. He started to feel something strange inside, and sometimes he could hear something. It called to him.

One night, he woke up suddenly. He could hear the call loudly, and it came from the woods. It was a long, sad howl and it didn't come from a dog.

Buck jumped up and ran through the camp into the woods. He walked slowly through the trees and, in an open place, he saw a **wolf**.

He walked slowly and carefully to the wolf. But the wolf was afraid of Buck and it quickly ran away. Buck ran after it and followed it through the trees. After an hour, the wolf understood. Buck didn't want to hurt him.

wolf /wʊlf/ (n) A *wolf* is a wild animal like a big dog.

49

They started to play. Then they ran for a long time. Buck followed the wolf. He was very happy with his new wolf-brother.

They stopped at a river and had a drink. But when he saw the river, Buck remembered Thornton. He couldn't follow his new brother. He had to go back to the camp. So, he turned around and started to run back. But the wolf wasn't happy. For an hour, he cried and ran next to Buck. But Buck didn't stop. The wolf sat down and howled sadly. But Buck had to leave him.

When Buck saw Thornton in the camp, he quickly jumped on him. He played games with him.

"Where were you, you crazy dog?" laughed Thornton.

For two days and two nights, Buck never left the camp, and he was always near Thornton. He followed him everywhere. Buck was next to Thornton when he slept. He stayed with him when he ate. He watched him at work.

But then he heard the call in the woods again, and it was loud. Buck remembered his wild brother. He couldn't eat or sleep.

Buck started to walk through the woods again, and he tried to find his new brother. But he didn't hear his sad howl again.

Then Buck began to sleep in the woods at night, and he stayed away from the camp for two or three days.

He fished in the river for food, and one day he killed a large, dangerous animal. It was a long and difficult fight but Buck won. He could live in the wild now, and he was strong, young, and intelligent.

"Buck is the best dog in the world," said John Thornton one day to his friends. "Watch him walk."

"Yes, he really is a wonderful animal," said Pete.

"You know, you're right," said Hans.

Buck walked out of the camp.

But Thornton and his friends didn't see the new Buck when he got to the trees. In the woods, he wasn't a sledge dog. In the trees, he was a wild animal—quick and careful. He could catch and kill anything. He killed many times and he always ate the meat of the dead animals.

◆

The weather got colder, and **moose** started to come into Buck's woods. Buck killed a small moose, but he wanted to kill an older, larger animal. Then Buck found one. He was a very big, strong moose, and he was very angry. He was angry because he had a big **arrow** in his back. He cried angrily when he saw Buck.

moose /muːs/ (n) A *moose* is a big North American animal with a head like a horse.
arrow /ˈærəʊ/ (n) An *arrow* is long, thin and often made from wood. You shoot it at people or animals.

Buck followed the old moose everywhere. Many younger moose tried to attack Buck, but he was fast. They couldn't catch him. When night came, the younger moose had to move away from the trees. They couldn't help the old moose now, so they left him.

Hour after hour, and day after day, Buck followed the old moose. And when the moose tried to eat or drink, Buck attacked him. The moose got weaker and weaker because Buck was always there. At the end of the fourth day, Buck pulled the tired moose down to the ground.

For a day and a night, Buck stayed by the dead animal. He ate and slept. Then he went back to the camp, to his friend, Thornton.

Three kilometers from the camp, Buck began to feel very strange. Something was different and he didn't like it. So he started to run quickly and he stopped outside the camp. He couldn't hear any birds or the sounds of his friends.

Suddenly, he found Nig, his little doctor. Nig had a large arrow in his back, and he was dead. Then he found Hans. He was on the ground and he had arrows in his back. He didn't move—he was dead, too.

Buck looked out from the trees. A loud, angry bark came from him, but he didn't hear it. For the last time in his life, he went crazy. He went crazy because of his love for Thornton.

Strange men danced in the middle of the camp. They heard the strange, loud bark. Then they saw a large, angry animal. It jumped at them from the trees. It was Buck, and he wanted to kill them.

He quickly killed the first man, but he didn't stop. He attacked them again and again, and the men couldn't stop him. They tried to kill him with their arrows. But he moved very quickly, so they couldn't catch him. They were afraid, and they ran into the woods.

But Buck hated them more than anything in the world, and he followed them. He killed two more men, but the others ran away.

Then Buck slowly walked back into the quiet camp and he found Pete. Pete was dead in his bed. Buck walked to the river of gold. It was red now. Skeet had his front legs and his head under the water.

And Thornton was also there, under the water. Buck couldn't see him, but he knew. John Thornton was dead.

Buck stayed next to the river all day.

Now he couldn't play with his friend or look into his eyes with love. Buck couldn't howl or cry. He felt a very bad pain inside, and it didn't go away.

But sometimes he looked away from the river and saw the dead Indians. They hurt him, and he killed them. Now he wasn't afraid of men, with their clubs and arrows. Buck felt strong and dangerous.

The sun went down and the sounds of night came to him. He walked to the center of the camp and listened. It was the call, and it was strong and beautiful. And for the first time, he was ready to answer it. Buck only loved one man—Thornton—and now he was dead. Now Buck didn't want the harness or the work of men. He never wanted to live with men again.

Suddenly, a lot of wolves ran into the camp. They stopped when they saw Buck. Buck was larger and stronger than they were. They were afraid.

Then one wolf jumped. But Buck attacked him and broke his thin neck easily.

Three more wolves tried to attack him. But Buck attacked their necks and faces, and they quickly fell back.

Then the other wolves ran at Buck and attacked him. But Buck was very strong and he fought well. They hurt him, but he didn't fall.

After half an hour, the wolves got tired and sat down. A thin, gray wolf carefully walked up to Buck, and he was friendly. It was Buck's wild brother from the woods, and Buck looked at him happily.

Then an old wolf stood in front of Buck and looked at Buck for a long time. He sat down and howled. Buck understood. The call was here, and he had to answer. So, Buck sat down and howled, too.

The other wolves came to Buck and barked at him in a half-friendly way. Then the wolves jumped away and ran into the trees. And Buck ran with them, next to his wild brother. He answered the call of the wild.

But the story of Buck doesn't end here. The Indians in the East began to talk about a strange dog. The dog lived with the wolves, but he wasn't a wolf. People were afraid of this dangerous dog. It took food from their houses and killed their dogs. Some people went out and never came back.

Every fall, these people followed the moose into the woods. But they never went to a place between two small mountains, with a river of gold in the middle. That place had a bad name, and people stayed away.

But there was one visitor to the place every summer. He was a great, beautiful wolf—but not a wolf. He came out of the green woods and went to the open place. He stopped next to the gold river and sat for a long time. Then he howled sadly, and left.

But in the long winter nights, he wasn't sad. He ran with his wild brothers, and he howled happily. He sang the song of the wild.

1 **Look at the pictures. What happened? Ask and answer questions. Work with another student.**

Student A: You are Thornton's brother. You are in the North and you are looking for Thornton.

Student B: You work in the North. You know about the last months of Thornton's life.

A: So you know my brother?

B: Oh, don't you know? I'm very sorry but …

2 **Discuss these questions with other students.**

A lot of animals do work for people. Which animals work in your country? What work do they do? Do you think they enjoy it? Is it right? What do you think?

You arrived in the North yesterday with your friend. You want to find gold and next week you are going to go into the wild. What do you have to buy for your trip? Think about food, clothes, the sledge, dangerous people, and animals. Write twenty things.

To buy

1 **Work with two or three other students.**

People went to the north of North America because they wanted to get rich fast. Most people wanted to find gold, but other people made money in different ways. What other ways can you think of?

> ....
>
> ....
>
> ....
>
> ....
>
> ....
>
> ....
>
> ....

2 **Read about a famous Yukon person. She made a lot of money in the North. How did she do it? Use the Internet and learn more about her.**

Have this conversation.

| **Students A–C:** | You work for newspapers. Ask Mrs. Mulrooney about her life in Dawson. What went right for her? |

| **Student D:** | You are Mrs. Mulrooney. Answer the questions. |

Belinda Mulrooney arrived in Dawson in 1897. She bought clothes and hot water bottles for $5,000 in the South and sold them in the Yukon for $30,000. With the money, she opened a restaurant and Dawson's best hotel, and also made $1,000 a day from gold. She was one of Dawson's richest women.

Write an advertisement for one of these:

- rooms at Mrs. Mulrooney's hotel
- warm clothes and/or hot water bottles

Or look back at Exercise 1 and choose one of your ideas.

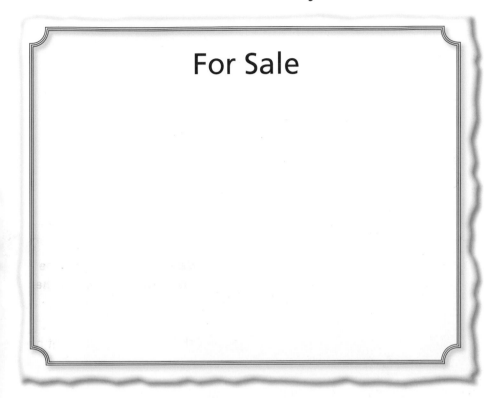

For Sale

How did these people get rich quickly? What did they do? Discuss these questions.

Ronaldinho   J. K. Rowling   Bill Gates

Think of other ideas. What can you do? Choose one idea.

5 **Write a letter to a friend about your idea.**

....

....

....

....

....

Dear .... ,

....

My friends and I have an idea! We are going to ....

....

....

....

....

....

....

....

....

....

....

....

....

With best wishes, ...

....